Peabody Institute Library, Peabody

SO-AZE-292

JUL - - 2004

U.S. WARS

OPERATION IRAQI FREEDOM

A MyReportLinks.com Book

Jeff C. Young

MyReportLinks.com Books

an imprint of

Enslow Publishers, Inc.

Box 398, 40 Industrial Road
Berkeley Heights, NJ 07922
USA

To my niece, Kelly Denise Smith

MyReportLinks.com Books, an imprint of Enslow Publishers, Inc. MyReportLinks is
a trademark of Enslow Publishers, Inc.

Copyright © 2003 by Enslow Publishers, Inc.

All rights reserved.

No part of this book may be reproduced by any means
without the written permission of the publisher.

Library of Congress Cataloging-in-Publication Data

Young, Jeff C., 1948–
  Operation Iraqi Freedom / Jeff C. Young.
    p. cm. — (U.S. wars)
Summary: Discusses the rise to power of Saddam Hussein and the threat
posed by his dictatorial regime, the events leading to the United States
attack on Iraq, and the aftermath of that conflict.
Includes bibliographical references and index.
  ISBN 0-7660-5088-2
  1. Iraq War, 2003—Juvenile literature. [1. Iraq War, 2003. 2.
Iraq—Foreign relations—United States. 3. United States—Foreign
relations—Iraq.] I. Title. II. Series.
  DS79.763.Y68 2003
  956.7044'3—dc22

                              2003013767

Printed in the United States of America

10 9 8 7 6 5 4 3 2 1

To Our Readers:
Through the purchase of this book, you and your library gain access to the Report Links that specifically back
up this book.
The Publisher will provide access to the Report Links that back up this book and will keep these Report Links
up to date on **www.myreportlinks.com** for three years from the book's first publication date.
We have done our best to make sure all Internet addresses in this book were active and appropriate when we
went to press. However, the author and the Publisher have no control over, and assume no liability for, the
material available on those Internet sites or on other Web sites they may link to.
The usage of the MyReportLinks.com Books Web site is subject to the terms and conditions stated on the
Usage Policy Statement on **www.myreportlinks.com**.
A password may be required to access the Report Links that back up this book. The password is found on the
bottom of page 4 of this book.
Any comments or suggestions can be sent by e-mail to comments@myreportlinks.com or to the address on
the back cover.

Photo Credits: AP/Wide World Photos, p. 13; BBC News, p. 30; Cable News Network, p. 44; CBS
News, p. 36; © Corel Corporation, p. 3; George Bush Presidential Library, p. 21; MSN News, p. 40;
MyReportLinks.com Books, p. 4; The Perry Castañeda Map Collection, The University of Texas
Libraries, p. 15; U.S. Air Force, p. 42; U.S. Army, p. 38; U.S. Department of Defense, pp. 16, 18, 23,
25, 28, 32, 45; U.S. Department of State, p. 26; U.S. Navy, pp. 1, 34; *Washington Post*, p. 11.

Cover Photo: U.S. Department of Defense

Cover Description: Soldiers from the 3rd Infantry Division line up in their firing position as they
await an enemy advance. This photo was taken March 24, 2003 in Southern Iraq.

Contents

MyReportLinks.com Books
Great Books, Great Links, Great for Research!

MyReportLinks.com Books present the information you need to learn about your report subject. In addition, they show you where to go on the Internet for more information. The pre-evaluated Report Links that back up this book are kept up to date on **www.myreportlinks.com**. With the purchase of a MyReportLinks.com Books title, you and your library gain access to the Report Links that specifically back up that book. The Report Links save hours of research time and link to dozens—even hundreds—of Web sites, source documents, and photos related to your report topic.

Please see "To Our Readers" on the Copyright page for important information about this book, the MyReportLinks.com Books Web site, and the Report Links that back up this book.

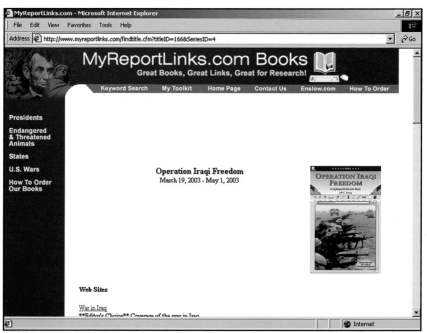

Access:

The Publisher will provide access to the Report Links that back up this book and will try to keep these Report Links up to date on our Web site for three years from the book's first publication date. Please enter **AOI1637** if asked for a password.

Report Links

 The Internet sites described below can be accessed at
http://www.myreportlinks.com

*EDITOR'S CHOICE

▶ War in Iraq
At this CNN Web site you can explore coverage of the 2003 war in
Iraq. Learn about the weapons used, coalition forces, Iraqi forces,
and much more.

Link to this Internet site from http://www.myreportlinks.com

*EDITOR'S CHOICE

▶ The War Behind Closed Doors
At this PBS Web site, *Frontline* explores George W. Bush's decision to
go to war with Iraq. Here you will find opinions, interviews, and a
chronology of events leading up to the "Bush Doctrine."

Link to this Internet site from http://www.myreportlinks.com

*EDITOR'S CHOICE

▶ Operation Iraqi Freedom
At the official United States Army Web site you can learn about
Operation Iraqi Freedom. Examine recent headlines, links to military
resources, and images from the war.

Link to this Internet site from http://www.myreportlinks.com

*EDITOR'S CHOICE

▶ Renewal in Iraq
At the official White House Web site you can read the latest news
dealing with Iraq, including presidential remarks, updates, and
briefings. You will also learn about the coalition and its global message.

Link to this Internet site from http://www.myreportlinks.com

*EDITOR'S CHOICE

▶ After Saddam
At this BBC News Web site you can read about the conflict in Iraq and
learn about postwar Iraq. Some topics covered are "Growing up in
Iraq" and "Who's Who in post-Saddam Iraq." You will also find images
and time lines.

Link to this Internet site from http://www.myreportlinks.com

*EDITOR'S CHOICE

▶ Jessica's Liberation
This news article from the MSNBC Web site, tells the story of how
Special Operations rescued Jessica Lynch from the hospital where she was
being held. There is also a description of Mohammed, the Iraqi lawyer
who assisted Special Operations in finding her.

Link to this Internet site from http://www.myreportlinks.com

 The Internet sites described below can be accessed at
http://www.myreportlinks.com

▶**Campaign Against Terror**
After the September 11, 2001 attack on America, the United States went to war with Afghanistan. At this PBS Web site you can read war stories, learn about the coalition, and view a chronology of events.

Link to this Internet site from http://www.myreportlinks.com

▶**Country Profile: Iraq**
This BBC News Web site provides a brief profile of Iraq. Here you will learn about postwar Iraq, Iraq's history, leaders, and the role of the media in Iraq. You will also find links to articles about Iraq.

Link to this Internet site from http://www.myreportlinks.com

▶**Fact Monster: Iraq Time Line**
Fact Monster provides a time line of Iraq's history from 1920 to the present. Here you will learn about the Ottoman Empire, King Faisal I, the Iran-Iraq war, and Operation Iraqi Freedom.

Link to this Internet site from http://www.myreportlinks.com

▶*Frontline:* **The Gulf War**
At this PBS Web site you will find oral histories and war stories, and you can learn about weapons and technology used during the Persian Gulf War. You will also find maps and a chronology of events.

Link to this Internet site from http://www.myreportlinks.com

▶**General Tommy Franks**
From the United States Central Command Web site you can read the biography of General Tommy Franks. Here you will learn about his military career. Click on "Galleries" to read briefings from Centcom about Operation Iraqi Freedom.

Link to this Internet site from http://www.myreportlinks.com

▶**George Herbert Walker Bush (1989–1993)**
At this Web site you will find a comprehensive biography of George H. W. Bush. You will also learn about key events in his administration including the Persian Gulf War.

Link to this Internet site from http://www.myreportlinks.com

Report Links

The Internet sites described below can be accessed at
http://www.myreportlinks.com

▶ George Walker Bush (2001–Present)
At this Web site you will find a comprehensive biography of George
W. Bush. Here you will learn about the first lady, his cabinet, staff, and
advisors, and key events in Bush's administration including Operation
Iraqi Freedom.

Link to this Internet site from http://www.myreportlinks.com

▶ Iran-Iraq War (1980–1988)
At this Web site you will find a brief history of the war between Iran
and Iraq. Here you will learn about the causes of the war, how it ended,
and what was learned.

Link to this Internet site from http://www.myreportlinks.com

▶ Iraq: After Saddam
From CBS News, you can learn about the situation in Iraq since the end
of the fighting. Read news articles and view postwar photos and videos.

Link to this Internet site from http://www.myreportlinks.com

▶ Iraq and the War on Terrorism
At the *Washington Post* Web site you will find a discussion about Iraq and
its connections to terrorism. You will also find links to discussions about
war in Iran, Somalia, Kashmir, Afghanistan, Pakistan, and the Philippines.

Link to this Internet site from http://www.myreportlinks.com

▶ Iraq Crisis
From the Military Analysis Web site you will find resources on the war
in Iraq including news and archives, targets, current weather, and
additional links.

Link to this Internet site from http://www.myreportlinks.com

▶ The Iraqi Ba'ath Party
At this BBC News Web site you will find an article that traces the history
of the Iraqi Ba'ath party. Here you will learn about the key members, the
party's origins, and the dismantling of the party.

Link to this Internet site from http://www.myreportlinks.com

Report Links

 The Internet sites described below can be accessed at
http://www.myreportlinks.com

▶ **The Long Road to War**
PBS's *Frontline* provides a comprehensive look at the United States
relationship with Iraq from 1990 to the present. Here you will learn how three
presidents dealt with Saddam Hussein in the past twelve years, and the causes
of the war with Iraq in 2003.

Link to this Internet site from http://www.myreportlinks.com

▶ **The New Iraq**
At this CNN Web site you can explore stories related to postwar Iraq. Topics
include the "Transition of Power," "Life After War," "Rebuilding Iraq," and
"War in Iraq."

Link to this Internet site from http://www.myreportlinks.com

▶ **Operation Desert Fox**
At this Web site you will learn about Operation Desert Fox. This includes an
overview of the operation, the defense policy toward Iraq, a map of Iraq, and a
chronology of events. You will also find additional articles, briefings, fact
sheets, and Web sites.

Link to this Internet site from http://www.myreportlinks.com

▶ **Organization of the Petroleum Exporting Countries**
At the Organization of the Petroleum Exporting Countries Web site you can
learn about the organization and its history. You will also learn about the
member countries, which consist of eleven countries that produce and export
oil in Africa, Asia, the Middle East, and Latin America.

Link to this Internet site from http://www.myreportlinks.com

▶ **Secretary of State Colin L. Powell**
At the U.S. Department of State Web site you can read the biography of
Colin L. Powell. You can also learn about Powell's political views, travels, and
view a photo gallery.

Link to this Internet site from http://www.myreportlinks.com

▶ **September 11, 2001: Attack on America**
At the Avalon Project at Yale Law School Web site you will find a collection of
documents related to September 11. This includes executive orders,
proclamations, determinations, and public laws.

Link to this Internet site from http://www.myreportlinks.com

Report Links

 The Internet sites described below can be accessed at
http://www.myreportlinks.com

▶ **Special Edition: Iraqi History Series**
At this Web site you will find a comprehensive history of Iraq in three parts. Part one covers Iraq after World War I, part two, the rise of Saddam Hussein, and part three, the United States relationship with Iraq.

Link to this Internet site from http://www.myreportlinks.com

▶ **United Nations Cyber School Bus**
The United Nations Cyber School Bus Web site is a tool young people can use to learn about the United Nations. Explore the United Nations history, participating countries, and much more.

Link to this Internet site from http://www.myreportlinks.com

▶ **UN News Centre: Iraq**
At the United Nations news Web site you can read the latest news regarding Iraq. Here you will learn about the United Nations Humanitarian Food Effort and recent developments in their involvement in Iraq.

Link to this Internet site from http://www.myreportlinks.com

▶ **USS *Abraham Lincoln***
At the official Web site of the USS *Abraham Lincoln* there are images of George W. Bush visiting the ship and meeting its crew members.

Link to this Internet site from http://www.myreportlinks.com

▶ **William Jefferson Clinton (1993–2001)**
At this Web site you will find a comprehensive biography of Bill Clinton. Here you will learn about key events in his administration, including Operation Desert Fox.

Link to this Internet site from http://www.myreportlinks.com

▶ **Worldwide Antiwar Protests Continue**
At this CBS News Web site you can read an article about antiwar protests throughout the world. You will also find a link to full coverage of the antiwar movement before and during the war.

Link to this Internet site from http://www.myreportlinks.com

Operation Iraqi Freedom Facts

▷ List of Combatants
Iraq *vs.* United States; Great Britain; coalition of forces including Poland, Australia, and ethnic minorities in Iraq.

▷ Time Line
1918—British troops take Mesopotamia after World War I.

1920—Iraq is placed under British control by the League of Nations.

1921—King Faisal I becomes Iraq's first monarch.

1932—Iraq becomes an independent state.

1979—July 16: Saddam Hussein becomes president of Iraq.

1990—August 2: Iraq invades Kuwait and establishes military control.

—*Nov. 29:* UN Security Council passes Resolution 678 authorizing use of "all necessary means" to force Iraq out of Kuwait if Iraq does not leave by January 15, 1991.

1991—*Feb. 27:* Kuwait is liberated by U.S.-led coalition forces.

—*April 3:* Iraq agrees to cease-fire terms of UN Resolution 687, which calls for removal of Iraq's weapons of mass destruction.

—*June 23 to 28:* Iraq fires shots to prevent UN weapons inspectors from intercepting vehicles carrying nuclear-related equipment.

1996—July 1: For first time, Iraq admits to having a program of chemical weapons, but denies having any usable weapons.

1997—*Oct. 29:* American weapons inspectors are expelled from Iraq.

1998—*Oct. 31:* Iraq ceases to cooperate with UN weapons inspectors.

—*Dec. 16:* U.S. and Britain launch Operation Desert Fox, bombing targets in Iraq believed to be used in the manufacture and storage of nuclear, chemical, and biological weapons.

2000—Iraq rejects new weapons inspections proposals.

2002—*Sept. 12:* U.S. President George W. Bush addressed the UN in an attempt to build a new multination coalition against Iraq.

—*November:* UN weapons inspectors return to Iraq.

2003—*March 17:* President Bush delivers a nationwide television address giving Saddam and his two sons 48 hours to leave Iraq or face military action.

—*March 19:* Operation Iraq Freedom begins with massive bombing attacks on Baghdad and other selected sites.

—*May 1:* In a speech delivered aboard the aircraft carrier USS *Abraham Lincoln*, President Bush announces: "Major combat operations in Iraq have ended."

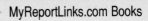
A Ruthless Dictator

On July 16, 1979, Saddam Hussein took over as the president of Iraq. Not even all members of Saddam's Ba'ath political party were pleased to see him get control of the government. They wanted a nationwide election to determine who would lead Iraq. Saddam moved quickly, and decisively, to silence them. His job as the leader of the Ba'ath party's underground militia gave him all the military muscle he needed.

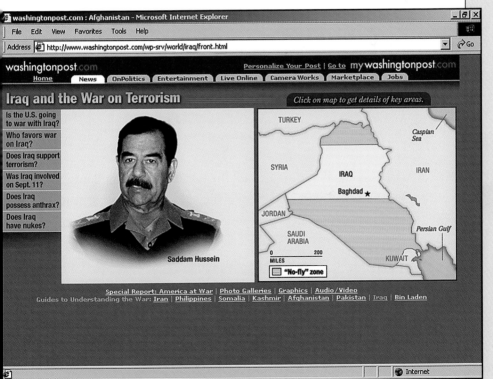

▲ In 1979, Saddam Hussein became the ruler of Iraq. He had eliminated his competition by using violence.

▷ A Violent Regime

On July 18, 1979, Saddam invited hundreds of party leaders and members of his Revolutionary Command Council to a meeting. It was at a large conference hall in Baghdad, Iraq's capital city. In the back of the hall, a video camera was secretly taping the proceedings. Dressed in his military uniform, Iraq's new president slowly walked to a lectern and began speaking.

Saddam announced that there were traitors in their midst who were seeking to overthrow him. After Saddam sat down, Muhyi Abd al-Hussein Mashadi, who had served as the secretary-general of the Command Council, walked out from behind a curtain. He had been secretly arrested and tortured a few days before this meeting. Now he publicly admitted that he was part of a Syrian-led plot to overthrow Saddam. Syria is a country that borders Iraq.

Mashadi began revealing names of his henchmen. One by one, the accused were escorted out of the hall by armed guards. After sixty accused traitors were removed, Saddam returned to the lectern. He wiped tears from his eyes and then repeated the names of the accused. The remaining party leaders trembled before they began applauding the new president. They were so grateful to still be alive, they heartily cheered and praised Saddam Hussein.

After all sixty were found guilty in secret trials, they were executed by firing squads. Before being shot, their mouths were taped shut. That ensured that none of them would utter any last words against the brutal new regime.

In the weeks that followed, Saddam tightened his grip on power by arresting, imprisoning, torturing, and killing many of cabinet members, government officials, and party leaders. People were turned in by ordinary citizens who

Saddam Hussein's appeals to the Iraqi people strengthened his power. He remained a ruthless dictator for over two decades.

responded to a hotline phone number broadcast on Iraqi television. Iraqi television was also used to broadcast the videotape of sixty accused traitors being led to their deaths.

Saddam's Youth

The son of peasants, Saddam Hussein was born on April 28, 1937, just outside of Tikrit, Iraq. Tikrit is a small city north of Baghdad. His father died before Saddam was born. After his mother remarried, Saddam ran away from home to escape his abusive parents. He lived with his Uncle Khairalla in Baghdad. Khairalla was an Iraqi Army officer who passed his anti-British and anti-Western feelings on to his nephew.

Chapter 2

History of Conflict

Between 5000 and 3500 B.C., most of Iraq, Syria, and the southeastern part of Turkey were part of what was ancient Mesopotamia. Many scholars credit the Mesopotamians with creating the world's first cities. Around 539 B.C., Mesopotamia became part of the Persian Empire, which includes what is now Iran. Over the next thousand years the area was controlled by many different peoples, until The Ottoman Empire took over the region in the 1500s. Mesopotamia remained part of the Ottoman Empire until the British gained control after World War I ended in 1918.

In 1921, the British renamed much of the territory that had been called Mesopotamia, Iraq. They established a new government. The British chose King Faisal I as the first monarch to rule over Iraq. Under Faisal's rule, the British still controlled Iraq's military, economy, foreign affairs, and oil reserves.

In 1922, British government leaders decided to redraw the boundaries between Iraq and Kuwait. The British hoped that by redrawing the boundary they could more easily maintain control over the region.

The newly drawn borders gave Kuwait about one hundred miles of coastline on the Persian Gulf. Iraq had claimed this territory. Kuwait also received two key islands on the Persian Gulf. This cut Iraq off from using the Persian Gulf for exporting its oil.

Ties to Kuwait

In 1961, the British granted Kuwait its independence. With the British leaving Kuwait, Iraq decided to claim the new nation as Iraqi territory. Iraqi Premier Abdul Karim el-Kassem claimed that Kuwait's agreement with Britain

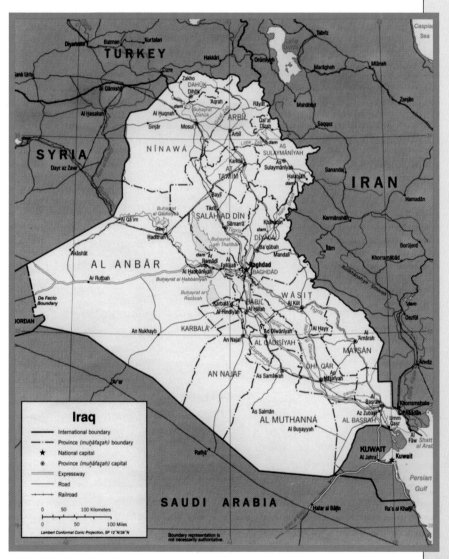

A map of Iraq. Baghdad is Iraq's capital city.

was a forged document that had been bought for fifteen thousand rupees.

Kuwait rejected Iraq's claim and asked Britain to come to their defense. Britain responded by sending nearly four thousand ground troops and air and naval support forces to Kuwait. The British buildup was also supported by the United States, Egypt, Syria, and Saudi Arabia. This show of force caused Iraq to back down.

In 1973, Iraq made yet another attempt to claim Kuwait. On March 20, the long-simmering border dispute erupted into violence. Kuwait immediately closed its border with Iraq and declared a state of emergency.

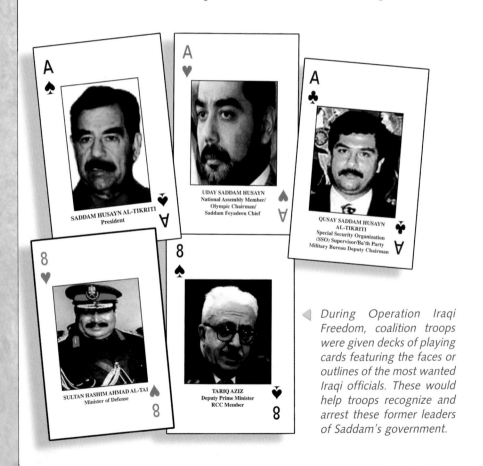

SADDAM HUSAYN AL-TIKRITI
President

UDAY SADDAM HUSAYN
National Assembly Member/
Olympic Chairman/
Saddam Feyadeen Chief

QUSAY SADDAM HUSAYN
AL-TIKRITI
Special Security Organization
(SSO) Supervisor/Ba'th Party
Military Bureau Deputy Chairman

SULTAN HASHIM AHMAD AL-TAI
Minister of Defense

TARIQ AZIZ
Deputy Prime Minister
RCC Member

◀ During Operation Iraqi Freedom, coalition troops were given decks of playing cards featuring the faces or outlines of the most wanted Iraqi officials. These would help troops recognize and arrest these former leaders of Saddam's government.

Saudi Arabia came to Kuwait's aid by sending close to twenty thousand troops to the Iraqi-Kuwaiti border. The Saudis' show of strength and the pressure from the international community caused the Iraqis to withdraw their forces from the border.

War with Iran

Iraq was at war with neighboring Iran from 1980 to 1988. It was a costly war in which anywhere from five hundred thousand to one million people were killed. It is well-known that chemical weapons were used in this war, which left many survivors sickened and diseased.

The Kurds

During the war with Iran, some of the Kurds, a minority people who live in Northern Iraq, had sided with Iran. When the war ended, the Kurds wanted to have their own homeland. They revolted against Saddam's rule. For a brief time, they controlled parts of Northern Iraq. The Iraqi army quickly put an end to the revolt.

Saddam ordered his army to use chemical weapons to subdue the Kurds. In the town of Halabjah in 1988, an estimated five thousand Kurds were killed when the town was bombarded by chemical weapons.

Repayment Dispute

Iraq's oil-producing economy was severely affected by the war with Iran. To pay for the military costs, Saddam borrowed money from Saudi Arabia and Kuwait. Both of those countries had secular (nonreligious) governments. Like Iraq, they were concerned that the new Iranian religious government headed by the Ayatollah Ruhollah Khomeini could start an Islamic revolution in their

▲ The oil industry has been at the center of many of Iraq's disputes. This oil field was set ablaze by Iraqi troops during Operation Iraqi Freedom.

countries. When the war ended, Iraq owed Kuwait close to $32 billion. Kuwait began pressuring Iraq for repayment.

Saddam thought that the Kuwaitis were ungrateful. He believed that Iraq had prevented Iran from invading and taking over Kuwait. He argued that $32 billion was the cost Kuwait paid for protection and continued security. Saddam also accused Kuwait of stealing oil from Iraq by slant drilling, which extracted oil from Iraq's rich Rumaila oil fields. When the Organization of Petroleum Exporting Countries (OPEC) leaders asked Kuwait to honor a quota and cut back on production, the Kuwaitis refused. This kept oil prices low.

Hussein wanted the price of oil to remain high so he could pay off debts to western countries that had supported his war with Iran. In addition, he was among those that believed that Kuwait should historically be part of Iraq. The United States and Britain had been two nations that supported Hussein's regime. Hussein felt that Kuwait was producing so much oil that it was keeping the price down. He knew if he took control of Kuwait's oil fields he could slow down their production.

Invasion of Kuwait

On the morning of August 2, 1990, Iraqi tanks and troops invaded Kuwait. Within a few hours, there were 100,000 Iraqi soldiers overrunning Kuwait's ill-prepared 20,000-man army. It took the Iraqis about seven hours to seize control of the tiny nation. On August 8, Iraq announced that it had annexed Kuwait, and the country was now a permanent part of Iraq. Many Western nations now feared that Iraq might try to take over Saudi Arabia. Hussein would then control their Saudi oil supply as well.

The day after the invasion, United States President George H. W. Bush reacted by freezing Iraqi and Kuwaiti assets held in the United States. He barred trade between the United States and Iraq. During his first formal press conference after the invasion, Bush implied that the Iraqis would be driven out of Kuwait.

"This will not stand," Bush said, "this aggression against Kuwait." When pressed for specifics, Bush replied, "Just wait. Watch and learn."[1]

International Cooperation

In the weeks following the invasion, the United Nations Security Council (UNSC) passed a series of resolutions against Iraq. The first resolutions placed trade embargoes and economic sanctions on Kuwait and Iraq. The Security

Council demanded that Iraq withdraw its troops from Kuwait. Iraq ignored the resolutions. On November 29, the UNSC passed Resolution 678, setting a deadline of January 15, 1991, for Iraq to withdraw its troops from Kuwait. The resolution gave Iraq "one final opportunity" to withdraw its forces, and authorized the UN to use of "all necessary means" to force Iraq out of Kuwait.[2] That resolution was also ignored by Saddam.

With the force of the UNSC resolutions behind him, George H. W. Bush began building a coalition of nations to support the United States in liberating Kuwait. Eventually, thirty-nine nations would support the United States. They supplied military and medical personnel as well as planes, ships, and tanks.

Once he was satisfied that the coalition was firmly in place, Bush then asked the U.S. Congress to approve the use of military force to oust Iraq from Kuwait. After three days, Congressional approval was granted. The Senate approved it by a slim 52 to 47 margin. The House authorized the action by a vote of 250 to 183.

▶ Operation Desert Storm

On the morning on January 16, about seventeen hours after the Resolution 678 deadline had passed, the coalition forces launched air and missile attacks on Iraq and Kuwait. Operation Desert Storm was underway. The coalition forces were led by United States General "Stormin'" Norman Schwarzkopf. Iraq responded by firing Scud missiles at Israel and Saudi Arabia. On February 15, Iraq offered to withdraw from Kuwait, but it placed too many conditions on its offer.

Operation Desert Storm ended with the liberation of Kuwait on February 27, 1991. Five weeks later, the

▲ At a private meeting at the White House, former President George H. W. Bush discusses the situation in the Middle East with the Emir of Kuwait on September 28, 1990.

UNSC passed Resolution 687. This laid out the terms of a cease-fire. The resolution declared in part that Iraq "shall unconditionally accept the destruction, removal, or rendering harmless under international supervision, of . . . all chemical and biological weapons and . . . all ballistic missiles with a range greater than one hundred and fifty kilometers . . ."[3]

This meant that Iraq was not allowed to have any weapons of mass destruction. These included long-range missiles, nuclear weapons, and chemical and biological weapons. (An example of chemical and biological weapons is putting the disease smallpox on a warhead so that when it explodes the people near it get seriously ill.) Within weeks, Saddam would defy this cease-fire agreement.

Chapter 3

Threat to the World

After the cease-fire was signed, there were hopes that Iraq would no longer be a threat to the peace and stability of the Middle East. The Iraqi military had been thoroughly routed. There were also hopes that economic sanctions put in place by the United Nations would keep Saddam from rebuilding his military. Many believed UN weapons inspectors would ensure that Iraq would disarm.

▶ Continued Disobedience

As early as March 1991, there were disturbing reports that Iraq was violating the terms of the UN-mandated cease-fire agreement. The agreement called for Iraq to end all flights of military aircraft. The use of helicopters was allowed only for nonmilitary purposes.

In at least fifteen different Iraqi cities there were reports of demonstrations against Saddam's ironfisted rule. Kurds in Northern Iraq and Shiite Muslims in South-ern Iraq were rebelling. Saddam used attack heli-copters to crush those revolts.

In the city of Basra, located in Southern Iraq, there were reports that Iraqi soldiers were firing on United States soldiers after the cease-fire was signed. There were no United States casualties, but it showed the United States and its coalition allies that they could expect an uneasy peace.

During the third week of March 1991, two Iraqi SU-22 warplanes were shot down by United States pilots for violating no-fly zone provisions of the UN cease-fire agreement. The attacks came after United States warnings

▲ *The United States Air Force had been involved in patrolling no-fly zones over Iraq, as well as being called upon to make bombing runs. Shown here is an F/A-18E Super Hornet taking off on a mission.*

that the use of military aircraft was regarded as a violation of the cease-fire agreement.

▷ UN Inspections

During June 1991, UN inspectors began conducting searches in Iraq for chemical weapons and missiles. During the week of June 23, 1991, Iraqi troops fired warning shots to prevent UN weapons inspectors from videotaping a convoy of trucks. The trucks were believed to be carrying electrical generators used to prepare weapons-grade uranium, an ingredient used for building nuclear weapons.

The Iraqis also began a pattern of turning away weapons inspectors from military bases and other suspicious

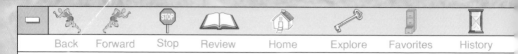
sites. Yet, the inspectors made some progress. They found and destroyed decoy missiles and launch-support equipment. They were also able to find chemical weapons. One inspection found Scud missiles fitted with warheads containing a powerful nerve gas. The number of chemical weapons they found was four times greater than what Iraq admitted to having.

Throughout the 1990s, Saddam's government continued to make it difficult for weapons inspectors to do their job. In 1996, Iraq finally admitted to having a program of chemical weapons. However, they denied that any of the weapons were functional.

▷ Violation of UN Resolutions

The United States, Britain, and France began denying Iraq access to its airspace. This would help to protect the Kurds in Northern Iraq and the Shiites in Southern Iraq. Both the Kurds and Shiites were ethnic groups not included in Saddam's political party.

Iraq objected to the no-fly zones as a violation of its rights to control its own territory. Both Russia and China backed up those objections. In December 1996, France ceased flying patrols in the no-fly zones.

The issue of weapons inspectors is more clear-cut, and Iraq's numerous violations are well documented. The Security Council tried to apply pressure by passing strongly worded resolutions. Resolution 949 demanded that Iraq "cooperate fully" with the weapons inspectors.

In 1996, Resolution 1060 demanded that Iraq grant "immediate, unconditional and unrestricted access" to sites designated for inspection by the UN. Iraq ignored it, and continued to block inspection teams from entering sites designated for inspection.

By October 1998, Iraq had ceased to cooperate any further with the inspection teams. The UN Special Commission in charge of weapons inspections removed all of their staff from Iraq. In a statement issued to the Security Council, Chief Inspector Richard Butler accused Iraq of obstructing the inspections, and failing to turn over documents.

▶ Operation Desert Fox

The day after the inspectors left, the United States and Great Britain launched Operation Desert Fox. The

Former President Bill Clinton launched Operation Desert Fox in 1998 to strike military targets in Iraq. The United States and UN had hoped the attacks would cripple Iraq's ability to produce weapons of mass destruction.

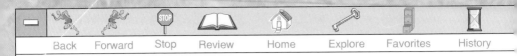
mission of the operation was to destroy suspected sites in the storage and manufacture of chemical, biological, and nuclear weapons. For four consecutive nights, United States bombers joined with Britain's Royal Air Force in a coordinated strike.

Air strikes ordered by President Bill Clinton targeted air defense and airfield facilities. Sites believed to be used for the production and storage of weapons of mass destruction were also targeted.

Clinton defended the action by reminding the world of Saddam's long history of obstruction and noncooperation with the UN weapons inspectors.

▲ Colin L. Powell was a professional soldier for thirty-five years, and one of the leading generals during the Persian Gulf War. In 2001, he became U.S. Secretary of State when President George W. Bush took office.

"The international community gave Saddam one last chance to resume cooperation with the weapons inspectors," Clinton said. "The Iraqi dictator has used these weapons against his neighbors and his own people . . . left unchecked, Saddam Hussein will use these terrible weapons again."[1]

The United States hoped that the air strikes would force Iraq to cooperate with the weapons inspectors and abide by the terms of the cease-fire agreement. President Clinton claimed that the air strikes had set back Saddam's long-range missile program by at least a year. Iraq claimed that bombs had destroyed hospitals, homes, and schools.

After Operation Desert Fox, there were still frequent violations by Iraqi aircraft flying in the no-fly zones. The Iraqis continued to fire surface-to-air missiles (SAM) and antiaircraft artillery at United States and British planes.

▶ Attacks on America

On September 11, 2001, an Islamic terrorist group named al Qaeda hijacked two commercial jetliners and crashed them into the twin towers of New York City's World Trade Center. Another hijacked flight crashed into the Pentagon building in Washington, D.C. Yet another plane was brought down in Pennsylvania before it could reach its intended target. It is estimated that over three thousand people died in these attacks. United States President George W. Bush linked Saddam's regime with supporting the al Qaeda terrorist network, led by Osama bin Laden.

The United States soon attacked the nation of Afghanistan which was run by an Islamic group called the Taliban. The Taliban were an extreme religious group which supported and allowed the terrorist group al Qaeda to set up training facilities in that country.

Chapter 4

The Fight Against Terrorism

Since 1990, the United States had named Iraq as a country that supported international terrorism. After the terrorist attacks on September 11, 2001, Iraq was the only Arab-Muslim country that did not condemn the attacks against the United States. In addition, Saddam sent money to support the families of terrorist suicide bombers in Palestine.

▶ A Call to Arms

The United States wanted to build a new coalition of nations to remove Saddam from power. United States President George W. Bush and Secretary of State Colin Powell made separate appearances before the United Nations.

△ *Since the end of the Persian Gulf War, the United States kept troops in the Middle East. Many were stationed in Saudi Arabia, and then Kuwait, before the launch of Operation Iraqi Freedom. This soldier mans a defensive position in Northern Iraq.*

Tools   Search   Notes   Discuss   Go!

On September 12, 2002, President George W. Bush linked Saddam's regime to terrorist activities in an address to the UN General Assembly. He further reminded them of Saddam's long history of defying UN resolutions he had pledged to obey.

Bush pledged that the United States would work with the UN, but if the UN did not back the United States, then the United States would act on its own.

"We will work with the UN Security Council for the necessary resolutions. But the purposes of the United States should not be doubted. The Security Council resolutions will be enforced . . . or action will be unavoidable."[1]

▶ International Dissent

In spite of Bush's speech, several key nations belonging to the Security Council were reluctant to go along with overthrowing Saddam. They were worried that overthrowing a sovereign government would set a dangerous precedent.

President Bush was more successful in getting the U.S. Congress to authorize the use of military force against Iraq. On October 11, by a vote of seventy-seven to twenty-three, the Senate approved a resolution giving Bush the authority to use American military power to enforce the UN resolutions ordering Saddam to disarm. The House of Representatives had previously approved the resolution by a vote of 296 to 133.

Four weeks after President George W. Bush received Congressional approval, Iraq agreed to allow the return of weapons inspectors. The United Nations passed a resolution on November 7, 2002 stating that if Iraq did not fully cooperate with inspectors, military action could be taken. There was a briefly renewed hope that peace would prevail and Saddam would finally cooperate fully with the weapons inspectors. On January 27, 2003, Hans Blix, the executive director of the UN weapons inspectors issued a report on how the inspections were going. In the end, it proved that although progress had been made, it still appeared that the Iraqis were not being truthful about their weapons program.

There was also hope that Congressional backing would help the United States receive approval from the UN Security Council. That did not happen. Three key member nations—Russia, China, and France—remained opposed to using armed force in Iraq. They were not alone in their opposition.

▲ British Prime Minister Tony Blair was President Bush's biggest supporter in trying to gain UN support for an attack on Iraq. British troops played a vital role in Operation Iraqi Freedom.

Opposition at Home

On February 15, 2003, antiwar activists held demonstrations to protest the impending war. Near the UN headquarters in New York, an estimated crowd of over one hundred thousand people turned out to protest military intervention in Iraq. Smaller demonstrations were held that day in Chicago, Los Angeles, and numerous other United States towns and cities. Polls showed that many Americans did not support taking action without UN approval.

Opposition Abroad

In London, police reported that a crowd of 750,000 turned out for an antiwar protest. In Germany, 500,000 turned out to protest. In France, there were scattered protests in sixty towns and cities. An estimated total of 300,000 people turned out for the French protests. Melbourne, Australia, reported the peace march there was the largest that city had seen since the Vietnam War.

France, Germany, China, and Russia were united in their opposition to the use of military force against Iraq. They argued that the weapons inspectors should be given more time. The United States argued that Iraq was not complying with the latest UN resolution, 1441, which called for Iraq to disarm itself of weapons of mass destruction and to cooperate fully with the weapons inspectors.

Powell Speaks to the UNSC

In yet another effort to win UN approval, U.S. Secretary of State Colin Powell addressed the Security Council to present the America's case against Iraq. During a seventy-seven-minute speech, he presented spy satellite photos and recordings of intercepted communications. Powell

said that United States intelligence had found thirty weapons sites that the Iraqis had cleaned out before weapons inspectors could get to them. He further claimed that Iraq had used mobile production facilities to manufacture biological weapons.

Powell was not able to sway the Security Council. Three countries—Russia, China, and France—held veto power over any action the Security Council could take. They remained united in their opposition to a military intervention. However, Powell's speech did increase American support for invading Iraq. A Gallup Poll showed that American support for military action increased from 50 to 57 percent after Powell's speech.

▲ Lance Cpl. Eder DelaCruz of the 15th Marine Expeditionary Unit fires a round of a 155mm howitzer during fire missions in support of Operation Iraqi Freedom.

Despite the lack of support from the UN, President Bush kept the pressure on Iraq. The same week that Secretary Powell addressed the Security Council, Bush ominously warned Saddam: "The game is over."[2]

Unilateral Action

On March 6, 2003, President Bush held a nationally televised press conference. The day before the press conference, France, Germany, and Russia announced they would block passage of anymore Security Council resolutions authorizing the use of military force in Iraq. Bush made it clear that the United States was ready to go ahead without them. He received support from British Prime Minister Tony Blair, as well as from Australia, Poland, and others.

"When it comes to our security, we don't need anybody's permission to defend the country," Bush said.[3]

Bush once again asserted that Iraq had links to the al Qaeda terrorist network responsible for the attacks of September 11, 2001. He said that war could be averted if Saddam would voluntarily step down and leave Iraq.

An Ultimatum

On March 17, 2003, President Bush addressed the nation and delivered an ultimatum to Saddam. The Iraqi dictator and his two sons had forty-eight hours to go into exile, or there would be war. As Bush spoke, there were 270,000 American and British troops and 1,000 warplanes stationed outside Iraq and ready for battle. President Bush also mentioned how the UN Security Council had failed to go along with the United States.

"The United Nations Security Council has not lived up to its responsibilities," Bush said. "So we will rise to ours."[4]

Chapter 5

Liberation

On Tuesday, March 18, 2003, Saddam appeared on Iraqi television. He wore a military uniform for the first time since the end of the Operation Desert Storm in 1991. He denounced President's Bush ultimatum as "despicable and reckless."[1] He warned his commanders and countrymen to prepare for battle.

Mohammed Aldouri, Iraq's representative to the UN, called the ultimatum "madness" and noted that this was

the first time in history that the president of one nation had ordered another to leave his own country. White House Press Secretary Ari Fleischer said that President Bush "still hopes he will take the ultimatum seriously and leave the country."[2] Fleischer added that if Saddam stayed in Iraq it would be "his final mistake."[3]

◀ *Tommy Franks takes a look around what used to be one of Saddam Hussein's presidential palaces. Franks was put in charge of the coalition forces in Iraq.*

▷ Iraqi Civilians Prepare for War

All through Iraq, lines formed at gas stations, bakeries, and airline ticket counters. International airlines canceled flights to Baghdad and other Middle East destinations. Tourists and foreign diplomats left Iraq as quickly as possible. Both the United States and Britain repeatedly warned the Iraqi military against the use of chemical or biological weapons.

▷ The Start of the War

On March 19, at approximately 9:33 P.M. est, Operation Iraqi Freedom began. For the first time in its history, the United States launched a full-scale attack without the enemy firing the first shots. General Tommy Franks was in charge of United States Operations. A combination of precision targeting and brute force marked the operation.

Satellite-guided Tomahawk missiles were launched from two United States warships and a submarine. They were aimed at "leadership targets." One of the first targets to be hit was a bunker where it was believed Saddam and his two sons had slept the night before.

Precision-guided bombs were dropped from Air Force stealth fighter-bombers. They were aimed at selected targets where Iraqi government leaders were thought to be hiding. Along the Iraq-Kuwait border, American and British warplanes flew bombing missions at targeted areas containing Iraqi artillery and surface-to-surface missile positions. They provided support for ground forces to begin moving in.

At 10:15 P.M., President Bush gave an address to the nation. In a brief speech he assured Americans and the rest

The rubble of what used to be Saddam Hussein's palace on Dora Farms. The United States hit this target early in the war in an effort to kill the Iraqi leader. It is unknown whether Saddam was hurt in the attack.

of the world that America's sole purpose was to remove Saddam from power and establish a democracy in Iraq.

"We have no ambition in Iraq, except to remove a threat and restore control of that country to its own people."[4]

President Bush added that since the war was on, victory was the only acceptable result. "Now that conflict has come, the only way to limit its duration is to apply decisive force. And I assure you that this will not be a campaign of half measures, and we will accept no outcome but victory."[5]

Bombing raids on Baghdad began on March 19, 2003.

The president received resounding support. On March 20, a *CNN/USA Today* Gallup poll was taken. Now, 76 percent of Americans were in favor of the decision to invade Iraq.

Shock and Awe

To ensure victory, the United States tried a new concept in waging war called "shock and awe." The battle plan is designed to destroy an enemy psychologically. Massive bombing attacks by precision-guided weapons are designed to destroy an enemy's will to fight rather than kill the enemy. The precision bombs were intended to reduce the amount of people killed in the cities. This was especially necessary because the Iraqi Army would hide weapons in places such as schools and hospitals.

Three days into the conflict, shock and awe bombing raids had reduced Saddam's opulent presidential palaces and multistory government buildings into piles of smoldering rubble. In fact, one precision bomb supposedly hit one of Saddam's palaces just moments before he left. The skyline of Baghdad was replaced by orange flames and black smoke.

On the ground, United States and British troops met light resistance as they moved toward Baghdad. The United States 3rd and 24th Infantry Divisions made it to within less than one hundred miles of Baghdad in just four days. Nearly ten thousand Iraqi troops surrendered in the first three days of fighting. The Iraqi military did not use either biological or chemical weapons to defend Iraq, as some had feared.

By April 9, American forces had reached Baghdad and were in control of the presidential palace and most government buildings. Within weeks Baghdad was secured

by United States troops. Meanwhile, British troops were occupying cities in Southern Iraq, giving out humanitarian aid to starving Iraqis.

Protection of Oil Fields

In Southern Iraq, the ground forces moved quickly to secure oil fields before the Iraqis could set them on fire. The Iraqis were only able to ignite a handful of oil wells. Iraq fought back by firing missiles at United States and British troops massing on the Iraq-Kuwait border. None of them hit their target, but they temporarily slowed down their advance into Iraq.

The main goal in Operation Iraqi Freedom was to carry out a short war with little fighting. Iraqi Major General Muhammed Thumayla surrenders his troops.

▷ Weakening of Iraqi Resistance

The bombing of Baghdad cut off communications between Iraqi military leaders in that city and commanders in the field. The powerful bombing also cut off electrical power and water to the city's residents. That further weakened the will of the Iraqis to resist the advancing forces. Sixteen days after entering Iraq, British and United States ground forces took control of Baghdad.

▷ Celebrations

As coalition forces moved into Iraqi cities, there was often celebration in the streets. Images of Iraqi people and children saluting and cheering for the soldiers filled television sets around the world. Statues and paintings of Saddam Hussein were torn down all over the country. Iraqi people scrambled for their allotment of the humanitarian aid packages being handed out by American and British soldiers.

▷ Coalition Setbacks

There were still setbacks. United States and British forces suffered twenty-two deaths in the first three days of the war. There were fire fights around the cities of Samawah, Basra, and Nasiriyah. Not all of the bombs avoided civilian areas. Iraq sustained an estimated 2,200 to 2,700 civilian casualties from the shock-and-awe bombing attacks.

After Baghdad fell, it became a lawless city. There was massive looting of the presidential palaces, government buildings, museums, libraries, and hospitals. Irreplaceable historical artifacts and rare books were stolen or destroyed. The looting continued even after the Baghdad police returned to work.

Jessica Lynch

The fighting also produced acts of bravery and heroism. One of the most notable was the freeing of an American prisoner of war (POW) named Jessica Lynch. Lynch was serving as a supply clerk when she and fourteen other members of her convoy were ambushed. This occurred along the main north-south highway leading into Baghdad, near the Euphrates River crossing of Nasiriyah.

Although she had just minimal combat training, Private Lynch shot several attacking Iraqi soldiers before

Jessica Lynch (left) and Lori Piestewa (right) were among those ambushed and held prisoner in Iraq. President Bush and Americans rejoiced when Lynch was found in a daring rescue attempt. Piestewa was killed in action.

emptying her weapon. According to the *New York Daily News*, Lynch "had her legs broken, one arm broken and at least one bullet wound."

While being held captive in a hospital in Nasiriyah, Lynch was spotted by an Iraqi attorney who was visiting his wife. The attorney, named Mohammed Odeh al-Rehaief, told Lynch he would help her. Mohammed walked six miles before he spotted a group of U.S. Marines. He told the Marines that he had important information about a woman soldier in a nearby hospital. After having Mohammed sketch some maps of the hospital, the U.S. Central Command (Centcom) formulated a plan to free her.

On the night of April 1, a joint effort by Marines, Army Rangers, and Navy Seals freed Lynch from her captors. It was the first successful rescue of an American POW since World War II and the first ever of a woman. Lynch was flown back to the United States for medical attention. Doctors have said that she does not remember any of her ordeal.

Unfinished Business

On May 1, 2003, President George W. Bush visited the aircraft carrier USS *Abraham Lincoln* as it was returning to San Diego. He addressed the crew and told everyone that the brief war was practically over.

"Major combat operations in Iraq have ended," Bush said. "In the battle of Iraq, the U.S. and our allies have prevailed. And now our coalition is engaged in securing and reconstructing that country."[6]

Rebuilding Iraq

Once the battles were over, the difficult tasks of rebuilding Iraq politically and economically laid ahead.

▷ Continued Military Presence

The United States has to maintain a military presence in Iraq until political stability is reached and law and order is restored. It is estimated that anywhere from 75,000 to 200,000 troops will have to stay there. Before democracy can flourish in Iraq, Iraqis will need to be convinced that

▲ On May 1, 2003, President George W. Bush addressed the world while aboard the USS Abraham Lincoln. Bush announced the end of military operations in Iraq and the end of Saddam Hussein's brutal regime.

Saddam is truly gone and that the Ba'ath party will not return to power.

There was no convincing evidence that Saddam and his sons were killed in the bombing attacks. On July 22, 2003 the U.S. confirmed Saddam's sons, Uday and Qusay were killed in a raid. Saddam still had not been found. Coalition soldiers were given playing cards that featured images of the most wanted Iraqis. These would help soldiers and officials recognize main offenders in Saddam's regime.

Many of Iraq's top government officials and leaders in business, education, and industry were required to join the Ba'ath party. Students at Iraq's top universities often had to join the party. A large portion of Iraq's most-educated citizens were party members.

Democracy Versus Theocracy

Iraq also has a diverse population, and the country has no history of democratic rule. Shiite Muslims make up 60 percent of Iraq's population. The Shiites have been very vocal in demanding that United States troops should leave Iraq as soon as possible. Already there are concerns that fundamental Shiite clerics could end the chance for democracy in Iraq by establishing a theocracy (a government ruled by religious leaders).

There are also large numbers of Sunni Muslims. About 97 percent of Iraq's population is Muslim. Other ethnic and racial groups include Kurds, Armenians, Assyrians, Turkomans, and Yazidis. All of these groups will expect to have a voice in the new government.

The United States' Role

Secretary of Defense Donald Rumsfeld said, ". . . how would we feel about an Iranian-type government running

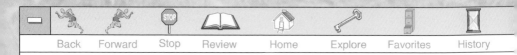

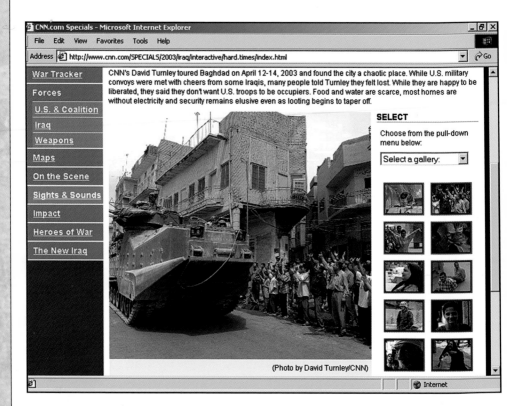

CNN's David Turnley toured Baghdad on April 12-14, 2003 and found the city a chaotic place. While U.S. military convoys were met with cheers from some Iraqis, many people told Turnley they felt lost. While they are happy to be liberated, they said they don't want U.S. troops to be occupiers. Food and water are scarce, most homes are without electricity and security remains elusive even as looting begins to taper off.

(Photo by David Turnley/CNN)

People celebrated in the streets in many Iraqi cities and towns when coalition forces drove the Iraqi military out of the area. Here, Iraqis salute United States troops.

everything in the country, the answer is: That isn't going to happen."[1]

American officials have said they can use Iraqi soldiers to rebuild roads and bridges and to hunt for mines. This would keep the former fighters gainfully employed. There are also plans to keep former government workers employed to run the schools and the health care system.

Estimates for rebuilding Iraq run as high as $100 billion. The United States does hold frozen Iraqi assets worth between $1 and $2 billion. There is also the possibility that the U.S. could dip into funds the UN is holding from

Iraqi oil revenues to defray rebuilding costs. Those funds amount to $11 billion or $12 billion.

The United Nations' Role

Another unresolved issue is what kind of a role the UN will play in rebuilding Iraq. Both President Bush and British Prime Minister Tony Blair have endorsed the use of UN humanitarian agencies in rebuilding Iraq. UN agencies such as the Children's Fund, the World Food Program, and the High Commission for Refugees may take an active role in providing food, water, shelter, and in meeting basic health needs.

Uncertain Future

Until United States troops can leave Iraq there will be increased resentment Americans by Iraq and much of the Arab world. Until a stable, inclusive, demo-cratic government is established in Iraq, United States troops probably will not be leaving.

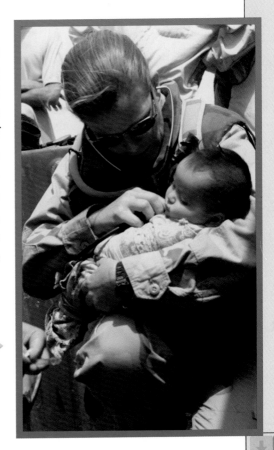

One of the main tasks for coalition forces after the battles ended was to provide humanitarian aid to the Iraqi people. Hospital Corpsman 1st Class Maureen Smith examines an Iraqi baby.

Chapter 2. History of Conflict

1. Peter David, *Triumph in the Desert* (New York: Random House, 1991), p. 46.

2. United Nations Security Council, "Resolution 678," November 29, 1990, <http://ods-dds-ny.un.org/doc/RESOLUTION/GEN/NR0/575/28/IMG/NR057528.pdf?OpenElement> (July 1, 2003).

3. United Nations Security Council, "Resolution 687," April 3, 1991, <http://ods-dds-ny.un.org/doc/RESOLUTION/GEN/NR0/596/23/IMG/NR059623.pdf?OpenElement> (July 1, 2003).

Chapter 3. Threat to the World

1. Linda Kozaryn, "Saddam Abused His Last Chance, Clinton Says," *U.S. Department of Defense*, December 17, 1998, <www.defenselink.mil/news/Dec1998> (July 1, 2003).

Chapter 4. The Fight Against Terrorism

1. George W. Bush, "President's Remarks at the United Nations General Assembly" *The White House*, September 12, 2002, <www.whitehouse.gov/news/releases/2002/09/20020912-1.html> (July 1, 2003).

2. Kevin Whitelaw, "Prosecutor Powell," *U.S. News & World Report*, February 17, 2003. p. 26.

3. David E. Sanger and Felicity Barringer, "President Prepares U.S. for War," *The (Lakeland, Fl.) Ledger*, March 7, 2003. p. A1.

4. Richard W. Stevenson, "Tyrant Will Soon Be Gone," *The (Lakeland, Fl.) Ledger*, March 10, 2003. p. A8.

Chapter 5. Liberation

1. John F. Burns, "As Baghdad Empties, Hussein Is Defiant," *New York Times*, March 19, 2003. p. A1.

2. Elisabeth Bumiller, "White House: Staying in Iraq Is Saddam's 'Final Mistake,'" *The (Lakeland, Fl.) Ledger*, March 19, 2003. p. A10.

3. Ibid.

4. "We Will Accept No Outcome But Victory," *USA Today*, March 20, 2003. p. 3A.

5. Ibid.

6. George W. Bush, posted as "President Bush Announces Combat Operations in Iraq Have Ended," *Renewal In Iraq*, May 2003, <http://www.whitehouse.gov/news/releases/2003/05/iraq/20030501-15.html> (May 8, 2003).

Chapter 6. Rebuilding Iraq

1. Robert Burns, "Rumsfeld says no to Iran-style rule in Iraq," *Orlando Sentinel*, April 25, 2003, p. A7.

Anderson, Dale. *Saddam Hussein.* Minneapolis, Minn.: Lerner Publishing Group, 2003.

Docherty, J. P. *Iraq.* Broomall, Pa.: Chelsea House Publishers, 2002.

Hughes, Libby. *George W. Bush: From Texas to the White House.* Danbury, Conn.: Franklin Watts, 2003.

Kotapish, Dawn. *Daily Life in Ancient and Modern Baghdad.* Minneapolis, Minn.: Lerner Publishing Group, 2000.

Nardo, Don. *The War Against Iraq.* Farmington Hills, Mich.: Gale Group, 2001.

O'Shei, Tim, and Joe Marren. *George W. Bush.* Berkeley Heights, N.J.: MyReportLinks.com Books, 2003.

Rivera, Sheila. *Operation Iraqi Freedom.* Edina, Minn.: ABDO Publishing Company, 2003.

Strait, Sandy. *What Was it Like in Desert Storm?* Unionville, N.Y.: Royal Fireworks Publishing Company, 1998.

Wheeler, Jill C. *Saddam Hussein.* Edina, Minn.: ABDO Publishing Company, 2003.

Index